DO YOUR OWN ARBITRATION

By Sadick H Keshavjee
LLB(Hon.)
TEP, CPS,(K)
CERTIFIED
ARBITRATOR

TRAFFORD
PUBLISHING™

Order this book online at www.trafford.com
or email orders@trafford.com

Most Trafford titles are also available at major online book retailers.

Printed in the United States of America.

ISBN: 978-1-4669-1612-8 (sc)

Trafford rev. 02/20/2012

 www.trafford.com

North America & international
toll-free: 1 888 232 4444 (USA & Canada)
phone: 250 383 6864 ♦ fax: 812 355 4082

This book is dedicated to the following, who, in one way or another, helped in my growth. My daughter Naveeda, and my son Nadeem, my late mother Sakina, my late wife Nuri, my sister Zarina, and my childhood friends, Dr. Sultan Kassamali and Dr. Mohamed Keshavjee. To me they are all alive even if in spirit

TABLE OF CONTENTS

vi

PREFACE

I have often, in my professional capacity, been told by parties to a dispute or even those involved in resolving such disputes that ADR in general, and Arbitration is such a daunting task and seems to be meant only for lawyers.

Whilst hiring a lawyer who has years of training is the ideal solution, in practical terms will this cost a lot of money (one has to pay for this expertise). More important one does not have to be a lawyer to be an arbitrator, be a party in an arbitration or assist such party.

In view of this I have found it appropriate to write this "Do it yourself" publication.

In addition I have come across lots of parties aiming not for justice but just revenge. My philosophy has been fight legally morally and ethically for your rights but to quote norman Vincent Peele "Leave revenge to God" or the universe whatever you conceive him or her to be.

I have interspersed such mundane but informative chapters with "Words of Wisdom".

I am looking forward to my favourite legal fictional thriller, John Grisholm, to write a novel based on arbitration where (in his usual brilliant way, we sympathise with the good guys).

I have endeavoured to show in the first chapter, that ADR in general and arbitration in particular is an alternative to the court. In the next chapter I show the historical development of this system followed by an outline of different forms of arbitration.

Then comes the meat. How an arbitration starts, the role of the arbitrator (and this includes the arbitration panel comprising more than one person).

After this, I discuss the written submissions emphasising all along that this process does not need rocket science.

After this comes a discussion on the hearing date and what happens here.

After this comes a brief outline on evidence 101 for the novice.

Of course next comes the award. A discussion follows as to what an award should look like And how it was arrived at. Unless it is properly made this award can be set aside. So, logically the next chapter discusses challenges to the award.

I then discuss the power of an apology. An interesting concept.

What follows are some principles of administrative law governing tribunals and thus arbitrators.

Then comes a brief table of statutory provisions governing arbitrations in 3 of what seem the busiest Provinces in Canada.

WORDS OF WISDOM

"Make me the instrument of thy
peace
Where there is hatred let me sow love
Where there is injury, pardon
Where there is doubt, faith
Where there is despair, hope
Where there is darkness, light
Where there is sadness, joy" - Gary
Zukav

CHAPTER 1

THERE AN ALTERNATIVE TO THE STRESS OF 'HAVING YOUR DAY IN COURT'?

The civil court, which in effect is a 'state controlled dispute resolution system can be one of the most tension packed event in one's life. But there are alternatives and now some eminent court judges are taking to ADR.

1. **What is ADR (Alternative/Appropriate Dispute Resolution)?**
   - 'A term for processes designed to settle disputes without formal trials'.
   - 'Replacing adversarial trials as a method of choice in resolving disputes'
   - 'To settle out of court is an attractive option for many and it is certainly the best approach and the results are generally fair' (Linda Dranoff 'Everyone's Guide to the Law').

2. **What is Arbitration?**
   - 'Arbitration is a procedure in which a dispute is submitted, by agreement of the parties, to one or more arbitrators who make a binding decision on the dispute'.

- 'In choosing arbitration, the parties opt for a private dispute resolution procedure instead of going to court'.
- A successful party can still go to court to enforce his or her ruling

WORDS OF WISDOM

"I am aware that I do not need to dominate anyone in order to be spiritually awake" - Wayne Dyer

"If you hate those who hate, you become like them" - Gary Zukav

CHAPTER 2

HOW THIS CONCEPT GREW - FROM HUMBLE BEGINNINGS

Historical Development;
Arbitration as we know it in the western world originated in England, when the sun never set on the British Empire.

Most tradespersons preferred to settle their disputes by arbitration in England, centuries ago. There were criticisms. But the criticisms were not directed at arbitrations as such. It was the way it was working.

So there has never been such a vast array of 'band aid' statutory interventions by Parliament as in this field, over the years in England. Today English arbitration law is a system that is the admiration of legal scholars and law makers worldwide.

➤ In the Canadian context

- Prior to 1986, the Arbitration Statutes of all the provinces were similar to, and were based on the English Arbitration Act of 1889.

- *The legislative (law enacted by parliament) and judicial (judge—made decisions) climate in Canada was not hospitable for arbitration of domestic commercial disputes at this time (prior to 1986).*
- *However, the 1970s and 1980s saw a worldwide trend toward the implementation of procedures, which would make the international arbitration of commercial disputes more feasible.*
- *These developments gave rise in Canada to the passage of Provincial and federal legislation relating to international arbitrations.*
- *The development of sensible rules for International arbitrations in turn led to reconsideration in many provincial jurisdictions of their laws relating to purely domestic arbitrations.*
- *In September 1995, four provinces (BC, Ontario, AB and Saskatchewan) enacted new domestic arbitration legislation. The Alberta, Saskatchewan and Ontario Arbitration Acts are similar, since they resulted from joint consultation whilst BC's is slightly different, having been enacted earlier.*
- *One of the many primary goals of lessening judicial interference has been accounted for by all of the new domestic arbitration legislation.*

- *All of the preliminary indications are that the courts are respecting the new domestic commercial arbitration legislation and interpreting it to minimize the scope of judicial intervention.*

('Judicial scrutiny of Domestic Arbitral awards' John Chapman)

In 1995 the Arbitration Acts of several Provinces adopted the Uniform Arbitration Act which gave further recognition to arbitrations and reduced court interventions.

WORDS OF WISDOM

"What can you say to someone that is so meaningful he will carry it with him unto death? Only a message from the heart can reach that deep, heal that powerfully and last that long" - Gary Zukav

"Blessed are the pure in heart for they shall see God" Mathew 5:3

"I know that my highest self is always needed to lift me up beyond the world I experience with my senses" - Wayne Dyer

CHAPTER 3.

IS ARBITRATION THE ONLY ALTERNATIVE TO THE COURT SYSTEM

There are other forms of ADR systems depending on the circumstances of the case
Comparing arbitration with other forms of dispute resolution systems:

Negotiation: An agreed process without the involvement of a third party. The parties themselves endeavour to reach an agreement on their own.

Mediation: A dispute resolution process where a neutral third party helps parties to make their own decision. The outcome is an agreement to which the parties are committed, when written into a contract and signed, it becomes final and binding.

Litigation in the courts: State sponsored resolution of disputes or 'going before the law. It is adversarial and past focused. The process is defined by rules. The court awards compensation punishment, the outcome often determined by public interest. Facts and evidence are presented applying the law to the facts. A solution is imposed by the courts.

WORDS OF WISDOM

"When the pain for continuing a destructive behaviour exceeds the pain of stopping, a threshold is crossed. What seems unthinkable becomes thinkable." - Gary Zukav

Advantages of:

Arbitration
1. It can be structured to suit the dispute
2. It is convenient
3. The arbitrator can generally be chosen by the parties, as long as there is no conflict of interest situation.
4. The arbitrator may facilitate negotiated settlement or mediation if required.
5. It is quicker than courts (if both parties committed to process).
6. It is generally less costly than courts.
7. There is privacy.
8. Awards are enforceable in courts.
9. Generally, there are no appeals.

Negotiation / Mediation
1. Parties participate in the process.
2. There is confidentiality.
3. It offers an opportunity for discussion.
4. There is an informal and comfortable atmosphere present
5. It provides for an ongoing relationship.
6. There is resolution by mutual agreement.
7. It is quick, economical, with over an 80% success rate.
8. Only an agreement resulting from a Negotiation or Mediation is binding

"How many times have you gotten caught in a circumstance, tried to pull away without taking time to assess your situation, and been injured? Sometimes your circumstances will not release until you stop, relax, and move with the flow. If you react to your circumstances without thinking, you make things worse." - Gary ZUkav

CHAPTER 4

. . . AND THERE ARE DIFFERENT SPECIES OF 'ARBITRATION'

Types of Arbitration:

There are arbitrations conducted only by documentation and this is catching on because it is less 'labour intensive'. Another type is 'final offer arbitrations, prevalent in the USA to resolve disputes as to players' salaries, on-line arbitrations, and a hybrid one called 'med-arb' which seems to be the most effective, providing for mediation, followed by arbitration for unresolved issues. Documents only

In Alberta, a hearing is not necessary unless a party requests one. The parties can therefore agree that the arbitration is to be 'documents only'. In addition to the type of documents normally produced in a lawsuit, evidence that would usually be given orally can be presented by way of sworn statements. This variation is popular in commodity and maritime claims and can be very cost efficient and time efficient for ADR between two cities.

a. Final Offer Arbitration

In this system, each party submits their final best offer. The arbitrator considers each offer and may choose one of those offers as an award, and nothing else. No compromise award is possible. Each party therefore has an incentive to make its final offer the most reasonable one.

b. On-line arbitration

In addition to incorporating the use of information technologies such as video-conferencing and document imaging into more ordinary arbitral proceedings, dispute resolution is available on the Internet especially when the matter can be documents only'. As a variation to this, the initial approaches can be made on the net after which the panel of arbitrators can be appointed and formal hearings can thereafter be facilitated.

"The overall field of dispute resolution cannot avoid being affected by the new information technologies because communication is central to this process. It is really with the advancement of the World Wide Web and powerful network based technologies that ODRs potential for both on and offline disputes began to be recognised".

(Extract from the book ONLINE DISPUTE RESOLUTION: resolving conflicts in Cyberspace by Ethan Katsh and Janet Rifkin 2001)

"There was clear evidence of trademark holders selecting arbitration providers that would likely rule in their favour, and identified disturbing trends in how certain providers allocated their cases. The first arbitration provider victim, Montreal based E—Resolution had to close its doors for good in December 2001, as it could not compete with rivals that tended to favour complainants".

"Complainants who are invariably trademark holders tend to select the two Arbitration providers: The World Intellectual Property Organization (WIPO) and the National Arbitration Forum (NAFA) who most consistently rule in their favour".

Second, the study found a significant difference in case outcomes when comparing single panel, where the Arbitration provider assigns single panel arbitrator, and three member panel cases, where the participants themselves largely determine panel composition. NAFA assigned 53%of its single panel cases to only six panellists who collectively ruled in favour of complainants

94 % of the time. WIPO meanwhile failed to assign any of its 1629 cases to two panellists, panellists who are generally viewed as more sympathetic toward domain-name registrants' (Extract of an article entitled CYBERLAW by Michael Geist in the Globe and Mail.)

" . . . In addition to incorporating the use of information technologies such as video conferencing and document imaging into more ordinary arbitral proceedings, increasingly more organizations are offering dispute resolution on the internet, especially when the subject-matter of the dispute is E-commerce or are Internet related such as domain name disputes . . . ."
In early April 2001 the CPR Institute for dispute resolution and Online Resolution Inc announced that they were forming a strategic partnership to develop new online dispute resolution tools for resolving business-to-business disputes.
(Extract of a paper by Jonnette Watson Hamilton, Associate Professor Faculty of Law U of C.)

c. Med-Arb. **(mediation followed by arbitration)**

This process is a combination of mediation and Arbitration. The latter deals with issues that cannot be resolved by mediation, and has been found to provide a lot of satisfaction and acceptance by participants.

The med-Arbitrator will explain to them that she will, as a mediator, try to assist the parties in reaching their own settlement, and if that does not work, the neutral will act as arbitrator and decide the unresolved issues for them.

It may be easier to carry on the med-arb if there is a three-person panel; the chairman or one of the panels can act as mediator, during which time the other two arbitrators can exclude themselves until the arbitration phase.

If it becomes apparent to the neutral that the parties would work out their own settlement which allows both parties to walk away, satisfied with the agreement, then so much the better. In litigation or arbitration, there is always a winner and a loser and often the winner also gets disappointed with the lawyers bill. This fact, coupled with the time, trouble and stress makes it worthwhile to resolve as many issues as possible prior to the arbitration. Whilst arbitrations are less formal than court proceedings, they are more formal than mediations and negotiations

The neutral must make it clear that anything disclosed in mediation must be brought before the other party if such disclosure will in any way affect the neutrals' decision in arbitration.

The neutral must also make sure that not only should he or she be fair and just but appear to be so, at all times.
This process is an advantageous one if handled appropriately

WORDS OF WISDOM

"We were born to touch each other.
What does your touch feel like to
others? Do you reach out in anger,
disdain or resentment? Do you need
to please, or need to push away?
Can you do what is appropriate, act
with an open heart and trust the
Universe." - Gary Zukav

CHAPTER 5

HOW DO YOU GET THE BALL ROLLING IN 'RIGHTING A WRONG'.?

Starting an Arbitration

All parties to a dispute must agreed to submit to arbitration either before a dispute has arisen, in, say a sale agreement or after the dispute has arisen.

Once a matter falls within the ambit of arbitration, the court will generally avoid interfering.

The agreement to submit to arbitration

The parties usually agree to send their dispute to arbitration by way of a written agreement to arbitrate.

The agreement usually sets out the nature of the dispute, the remedy the requested, the date of the agreement and the conditions under which the parties agree to be bound.

a) Estimated value of the claim The nature of the dispute in summary form.

b) The demand and remedies sought.

c) The "staying" that is, the holding off of any court proceedings whilst this arbitration proceeds

d) The obligation to provide all documents related to the dispute at hand.

e) The right of the arbitrator to appoint legal counsel, under certain circumstances.

f) The right to obtain an award in court, whether interim or after the final award is rendered.

g) No revocation of the power of arbitrator (except for (misconduct). Bankruptcy, insolvency, incompetence, or disability of the arbitrator will not generally prevent the arbitrator from acting.

h) The decision of arbitrator is, binding on executors, administrators, of parties

WORDS OF WISDOM

"Your painful emotions are designed to bring your attention to the parts of your personality that you were born to challenge and change, so that you can transform yourself from angry, jealous, avaricious, or vengeful person into one who is compassionate, wise and grateful for life." - Gary Zukav

THE REFERENCE

1. Variety of procedures

The arbitrator is entitled to adopt whatever procedure he thinks fit, provided that it does not conflict with the express or implied terms of the arbitration agreement. The presumption is that the effective business of the arbitration will be done at a single hearing at the conclusion of which the arbitrator will reach his decision only on the basis of what has been laid before him or her, and nothing else.

The adversarial system as practised in England and most common law countries is, (arguments by plaintiff and defendant in an all out effort to win) predominantly oral is character. Most evidence is given by witnesses who attend in person, although in certain circumstances it is permissible to use written statements in substitution.

Justice Spinoza has commented that in Canada decisions are increasingly based on written submissions

Preparation of a 'core bundle' of the principal documents, which the tribunal can usually be expected to have read before the hearing; the use of witness statements as the basis of their evidence, with each witness tendered for cross examination ; and the use of written proposition as the foundation of, although not a substitute oral argument on fact and law.

If the application of the rules governing conflict of laws(the rules deciding which country's law shall apply to the arbitration) indicate that the contract is governed by a foreign law, it is that foreign law that will govern the decision.

THE INTERVENTION OF THE COURT

Where the parties have agreed to submit their differences to arbitration, the Court is usually concerned only with the procedural aspects of the dispute. If the defendant wishes to rely upon the arbitration agreement, his remedy is to invite the court to abstain from exercising its jurisdiction, and to stay the action. If the arbitration breaks down, the Court can in certain circumstances resume its jurisdiction, and take the merits of the dispute into its own hands.

    a) The courts in most jurisdictions, have recognised the validity of clauses in an agreement which make it a condition that, to enforce a claim under a contract that the claimant must have taken the matter to arbitration and obtained a favourable award. Such a clause does not bar the jurisdiction of the Court, but it does provide a defence to the action, where a party fails to do this.

The court can order(a) the discovery of documents (production of documents to support a party's claim) to be verified by affidavit (a document signed under oath in the presence of a notary etc) ;(b) interrogatories to be answered on preservation of any fund and issue in the arbitration ; (d) the appointment of a receiver ;(e) the grant of an injunction.

The court will not act unless the matter complained of has created a real risk of injustice.

In the absence of a dispute (which has been understood as a meaning genuine dispute) the court will not order that the action should be stayed so that the matter can be referred to arbitration. The procedural consequences are important, for this principle opens the way for the plaintiff, even in a case governed by an arbitration clause, to employ the summary mechanisms of the Court where the defendant has no defence at all to the claim, or only a spurious defence. What happens is this. The claimant commences an action in the High Court, and states on affidavit his belief that there is no defence to the claim. The defendant must then respond, also on affidavit, showing reasons why he does have a defence. If the Court accepts the contention of the plaintiff, it will refuse to stay the proceedings and will instead give immediate judgement for the plaintiff. This abbreviated procedure, which is based entirely on documentary evidence, and which eliminates not only the usual preliminary steps in the action, but also the trial itself, provides a valuable means of obtaining relief by way of an alternative to a speedy arbitration.

2. In certain jurisdictions, claims can be barred because of a time limit placed by statute

3. The notice of arbitration serves to stop time from running against the claimant under any period of limitation which may apply to the claim, by virtue of a statute or an express provision in the substantive contract. The expiry of a contractual time limit is not, however, necessarily fatal to the claim. In particular, the Court often, has jurisdiction to extend a limit imposed by the arbitration agreement, if it considers that 'undue hardship' would be caused by treating the claim as time-barred

WORDS OF WISDOM

"One man's word is no mans word: we should quietly hear both sides" - Goethe

CHAPTER 6

'THE ARBITRATOR' - DEMISTYFYING THIS CREATURE

The arbitrator has certain rights and obligations. What follows should allow the reader a bird's eye view of this role

Duties of the Arbitrator

1. To provide a fair hearing
2. To resolve issues.
3. To make findings of fact, and draw reasonable conclusions based on those facts.
4. To write an award that fairly decides the issues based on the facts found and the arguments made.
5. To write an award that will not be easily overturned by the courts

The arbitrator acts like a judge albeit that this person does not need specialized training, and they do not have to follow decisions of other arbitrators. Some arbitration agreements require arbitrators to be knowledgeable in certain specialized fields.

Questions for the arbitrator

a) Do the terms of the arbitration agreement cover the dispute?

b) Does the arbitrator have the jurisdiction to hear the dispute?

c) How much money is involved?

d) Is there a potential conflict of interest?

e) Date when the award will be issued?

f) Will there be written reasons

Code of Ethics for arbitrators

1. An Arbitrator shall be fair.
2. Act with integrity.
3. Act impartially and independently.
4. Treat participants with courtesy, fairness and integrity.
5. Full disclosure to prevent an apprehension of bias.
6. Must be able and competent to accept the Arbitration.
7. Shall complete arbitration after the appointment.
8. Communicate equally with the parties.
9. Keep all matters confidential.
10. May act as mediator or conciliator (caucusing and 'suggestions' allowed)

WORDS OF WISDOM

"Practice moderation in all things except love" - Gary Zukav.

CHAPTER 7

PUTTING PEN TO PAPER . . . . WHO DID WHAT TO WHOM

This process is not rocket science. But it does require a clear thinking and common sense coupled with brevity. It should be like a mini skirt—long enough to cover the subject matter but short enough to be interesting.

PLEADINGS

The claimant is the person making the claim, and the defendant is the one defending the claim.

Pleadings are documents which set out particulars of the claim, defense and counter claim

STATEMENTS OF CASE

The principal means by which the parties identify the issues by provision of "pleadings" which is a term often used to describe any document prepared for this purpose. The pleadings can be

- Very formal documents which mimic the documents used in court; or
- "Statements of case" which are less formal and contain additional documents such as documentary evidence.

How does an arbitrator decide what sort of pleading is appropriate? It will depend upon, amongst other things.

- Any agreement made in procedural rules.
- The expectations of the parties-for example, where both parties are formally represented by counsel, traditional pleadings may be appropriate.
- The volume of documents which may be relevant.

The key thing is that the claimant's (and counterclaimant's) pleading, should contain a clear statement of (a) the nature of the claim, (b) the basis of the entitlement that is being claimed, (c) evidence which allegedly support the claim. Pleadings should deal with each of these issues.

The order of delivery of pleadings is ordinarily as follows:
1. Statement of claim
2. Statement of defense (and counterclaim)
3. Reply to defense (and defense to counterclaim)
4. Reply to defense to counterclaim.

Unless any agreed rules of procedure specify the intervals between pleadings, it will be for the arbitrator to decide after hearing submissions. The normal period between pleadings ranges from 2 weeks for a small case, up to 8 or 12 weeks for very large cases.

Request for particulars

Frequently a recipient of a pleading will complain that it lacks proper details. This party will apply for an order that the other party should supply further particulars. Where such an application is made, the arbitrator should test that the request fulfills the purpose i.e. To enable the opposing party to know what case is being made in a sufficient detail to prepare an answer to it. In recent years there has been a tendency to forget this basic purpose and to seek particularization even when it is not really required. Pleadings are not games to be played at the expense of the litigants, nor as end in themselves, but a means to an end, and that end is to give each party a fair hearing." (Mustill and Boyd)

The Arbitrator or the parties may consider the clarifications of the dispute will be of value. If so, the arbitrator will be in broad terms have a choice between four different procedures

34

(i) To order full pleadings, in the same manner as the High Court. These are written statements of the facts which the parties intend to prove in support of their respective contentions. They should contain only assertions of fact (at any rate in theory), and should not compare arguments, evidence or propositions of law

(ii) To order each party to deliver a full written statement of his case (10). Such a statement would include arguments and evidence, as well as bare allegations of fact; and embrace the issues of law as well as of fact

(iii) To order the delivery of brief informal letters setting out the parties' respective cases.

The choice between these various ways of clarifying the issues depends upon the nature of the dispute, the qualifications of the tribunal, and the general nature of the procedure expressly or impliedly agreed by the parties.

Pleadings are not the ideal way of isolating the essential issues in a dispute. An artfully drawn defense may conceal as much as it reveals. Even the most communicative of pleadings tells the reader little or nothing of the case which the party will advance on the issues of law, or the evidence which he will adduce to prove his allegations of fact. Moreover, the use of pleadings tends to multiply the issues, because of the natural desire of the advocate to keep open all his arguments and options until the last possible moment in the hope of some favorable turn of events. This means that a party who bases his preparation of the case on his opponent's pleadings may arm himself with evidence to meet a point which in event is never seriously pressed.

For these reasons, and because pleadings are believed to imply a legalistic approach inappropriate to commercial arbitrations, many lay arbitrators avoid them. On the other hand, when the properly used, pleadings can combine precision with the economy of effort in way which none of the alternative procedures can attain. Moreover, they have the great benefit of furnishing a ready-made procedure which all lawyers can understand.

(i) Written statements of case. As an alternative to pleadings in a strict legal form, it is sometimes ordered (3) that the parties shall each deliver written statements of case, setting out their contentions on fact and law. Such documents should be more informative than pleadings, since they contain propositions of law with supporting arguments, and deal with the facts in a less elliptical way than many pleadings. The advantage of a full statement of case is that the arbitrator is enabled to familiarize himself with the case at comparatively early state, thus saving time at the hearing itself-a course which is not usually practicable.

The Arbitrator may find it helpful to tell the parties - (a) approximately how long the statements are intended to be (b) whether they are supposed to be exhaustive expositions of the case, or merely summaries.

WORDS OF WISDOM

"The truth shall make you
free" - John 8:32

"To accuse others for others for one's
misfortune is a sign of want of
education

To accuse oneself shows that ones
education has begun

To accuse neither oneself nor
others shows that one's education is
complete" - Epictetus

CHAPTER 8

WHAT YOU NEEDED TO KNOW ABOUT THE HEARING BUT WERE UNWILLING TO ASK

STEPS IN THE ARBITRATION ADVOCACY PROCESS

Three key words are important, preparation, preparation and preparation!

i. One should determine what law and policies apply with regard to the particular hearing. (I.e. the enabling legislation, rules of procedure, as it is important to ensure that the tribunal has the jurisdiction authority and powers to conduct the hearing)

ii. Determine from the rules, stages in the process and deadlines

iii. Determine who makes the decision at each stage

iv. Determine the concerns of other stakeholders (parties not directly connected to the hearing, but that could be affected by this arbitration.)

v. - Tailor submissions
   - Identify issues questions of fact, what laws apply and the correct policy to apply.

(preliminary procedures, disclosure and legal research).

- Determine burden and standard of proof See chapter on evidence)

Collect evidence and identify witnesses with subpoenas if need be

- Research the law

- Organise materials. Binder indexed with book of authorities

- Never mislead the tribunal and do not take extreme positions unless provable.

Focus on the most convincing issues and arguments.

- Show respect.

- Address the tribunal.

vi. Obtain reasons for the decisions.

A useful acronym is KISS (Keep It Short and Simple)!

WORDS OF WISDOM

"One of the most striking differences between a cat and a lie is that a cat has only 9 lives - Mark Twain"

"I know I am strengthened as I seek to make truth my personal reality" - Wayne Dyer

CHAPTER 9

EVIDENCE FOR THE NOVICE

EVIDENCE IN ARBITRATION (Credit to Chartered Institute of Arbitrators of UK)

An arbitration is not a court hearing. The strict rules of evidence can be done away wit, by agreement of the parties. But an overview of the basic rules can be helpful so that you are not cough unawares, with a sneaky opponent.

- The arbitrator cannot, unless all parties agree, make him or her inquisitor (or "enter into the arena" as Lord Denning would call it. That is, only clarification questions should be asked and not conduct the hearing), the arbitrator should also not take evidence behind a party's back. The rules of evidence which are applied in the civil courts also bind an arbitrator unless the parties to the contrary. It is not open to the arbitrator to disregard those rules except by consent of all parties.

- Consent to a departure from the usual rules of evidence is most often expressed in the arbitration agreement itself, but can be implied from conduct and, sometimes, from the nature of the arbitration, especially if it is, say, a commercial arbitration:

- *In arbitration, the strict rules of evidence are usually relaxed by agreement.*
- *The courts will readily imply consent to modify the usual rules, or a waiver of irregular application of those rules, if a party fails, at the hearing, to object promptly to the admissibility of evidence which should ordinarily be rejected, and instead sits idly and attempts to take the first objection only on appeal from the award.*
- *There is nothing to prevent the parties from agreeing that more restrictive rules than those ordinarily applied in the civil courts should apply in their arbitration.*
- *Evidence must be admissible*
- *The most important category of inadmissible evidence is irrelevant material. Only evidence that is relevant to issues in the arbitration. Relevance depends upon the particular facts of each case.*
- *The arbitrator must take care to keep the hearing firmly focussed upon issues which have a direct bearing on the claim, and ought not to permit a marginal exploration into matters not connected. (i.e. go on a fishing expedition)*
- *The other main categories of inadmissible evidence are as follows:*
  - *Opinion evidence: the opinion of a witness is inadmissible unless he is an expert (by qualification or experience in that subject)*

- Hearsay evidence: in general, only facts within the direct knowledge of a witness are relevant, not those he has been told by others.
- Privileged communications: confidential documents passing between parties and their legal advisers.

The courts are reluctant to overturn awards on the grounds of the mere wrongful reception or rejection of evidence. Provided the arbitrator acts honestly and in a judicial manner (for instance, by affording all parties the opportunity to make submissions before he gives a ruling), he is not by reason of that ruling alone guilty of misconduct, even though the ruling may be contrary to law, at least if the error does not go to the root of the question he has to decide:

<u>Conditional admissibility</u>
- Questions of admissibility are normally dealt with by an immediate ruling by the arbitrator
  - In those circumstances he may admit the evidence "de bene esse", that is to say :on a provisional basis", so that depending on what later evidence reveals, he may eventually decide to admit the contentious evidence, or to exclude and ignore it in reaching his award.

Weight of the evidence

- Evidence that is admitted in arbitration must still be weighed by the arbitrator in order to determine how much force should be given to it. All the circumstances of the evidence and the manner in which it is given are material; but finally the arbitrator must bring his own common sense, experience and judgement to bear in order to decide, for instance, which of two conflicting witnesses is telling the truth, or what are the proper inferences to be drawn from the things he has seen and heard.

- Direct evidence of a fact is usually more weighty than hearsay evidence of the same fact, and is often more convincing than mere circumstantial evidence

- Circumstantial evidence can point just as clearly as direct evidence in favour of a particular conclusion.

- Expert witnesses led by one party may seem better qualified or more authoritative than those produced by the other.

- Witnesses who have a direct interest in the outcome of the arbitration may have to be treated with more suspicion than wholly independent witnesses.

- It is usually for the party making the claim in the arbitration to prove by evidence to the arbitrator's satisfaction each component part of the claim. The burden of proof is said to lie on the party asserting its entitlement to relief.

- If the evidence does not persuade the arbitrator on all the disputed issues then the claim must fail.

- If the evidence on an issue or in the claim is of equal value so that the tribunal simply cannot decide between the contentions of either side, then the party on whom the burden of proof lies must fail.

- Within a single arbitration there may well be issues in respect of which the burden of proof falls on different parties, for instance, the claimant may allege negligence and the respondent "contributory" negligence; the claimant may allege a contract and the respondent may allege its invalidity on the grounds of fraud, misrepresentation and mistake.

- Sometimes, a rule of common law, statute or an agreement between the parties will throw the burden of proving an issue on to the respondent:

- In theory, the burden of proof can be further broken down into the evidential burden, i.e. the duty to produce sufficient evidence from which the arbitrator may safely conclude that the thing contended for is true; and the persuasive burden, i.e. the duty to prove to the arbitrator's satisfaction that the thing contended for is in fact true.

- The practical importance of this distinction is that if the evidential burden is not discharged then that aspect of the arbitration should proceed no further, since there is insufficient evidence on which to base a finding of fact; and if it does proceed, the losing party may attempt to impeach the award on the grounds that the evidence was inadequate to support a finding on that point.

Standard of proof

- The standard of proof is the degree of certainty which the arbitrator must hold before finding that the burden of proof has been discharged.
- In arbitrations this is normally defined as the _balance of probabilities_. In other words, the party bearing the burden of proof must prove that the thing contended for is more likely than not to be true.
- Although expressed in objective terms, the standard of proof is applied in a flexible and subjective way in that the degree of certainty required for the arbitrator to be satisfied "on balance" will vary according to the gravity of the allegation made; the consequences of accepting it to be true; the probability or

otherwise of the allegation; the size of the claim; and so forth.

- Even if unlawful or criminal conduct is alleged, the arbitrator must not apply the criminal standard of proof "beyond reasonable doubt"; but must apply the "balance of probability" test, recognizing that it will be more difficult for a party to pass that test where serious allegations are made:

- Where no evidence is necessary things that are not in issue, either because they form the "common ground" between the parties (as will be apparent from the pleadings or statement of case) or because they are formally admitted need not to be proved by evidence.

- Things of which "judicial notice" is taken also need not be proved by evidence. Such things are deemed to be within the inherent knowledge of the arbitrator.

- "Notorious facts" may, for example, be judicially noticed, as being so well established that no sensible person could dispute them:

- Arbitrators may use their general knowledge of the relevant trade without putting the matters on which they rely to the parties

- If, however, the arbitrator has particular knowledge of the events which are the subject matter of the dispute, he is bound to tell the parties of that knowledge, so as to give them an opportunity to call evidence to support or contradict his understanding of the facts.

- Presumptions are substitutes or partial substitutes for evidence which entitle the arbitrator to pronounce without complete or any evidence on a particular issue. As such, they are aids to determination.
- The arbitrator may be obliged to find that a certain fact exists unless it is proved by evidence to the contrary that it does not exist:
- He may be obliged to find that a certain fact exists unless prima facie evidence in rebuttal is adduced to cast doubt on its existence:
- The arbitrator may be entitled (but not bound) to find that a fact exists. There is sufficient circumstantial evidence from which the fact in question may (but not must) be inferred:
  - Legal professional privilege
  - Communications between client and legal advisor

Such communications, whether oral or in writing, will be privileged from disclosure provided the following conditions were fulfilled at the time they were made:

a) The communication is made to or by the legal advisor in his professional capacity;

b) The person retained to advise falls within the classes of "legal adviser" recognized by the privilege:

c) The communication is made in connection with the giving or receiving of advise within the ordinary scope of the legal adviser's employ:

d) The relationship of client and legal adviser exists between the parties, or is in reasonable contemplation:

e) The parties intend that the communication remain confidential as between themselves:

Communications with third parties:

a) the communication was intended to be confidential as between the maker and the recipient;

b) Some litigation, whether civil or criminal, and whether in the ordinary courts or by arbitration, was in existence or was "reasonably contemplated" or "in definite prospect";

c) The dominant purpose for the obtaining or coming into existence of the communication was to assist in fighting that litigation:

This discretion subsists even where the party seeking to use the evidence has been guilty of no wrongdoing in obtaining it:

"Wrongful" inspection or copying of an opponent's privileged documents is however likely lead to the court issuing an injunction against the wrongdoer from using what he has obtained by that method:

Waiver of legal professional privilege

a) Legal professional privilege is a PRIVATE privilege. Thus it is personal and not proprietary. The client is therefore entitled to reveal to the arbitrator the contents of a communication in which he holds the privilege, and may sometimes be deemed to have made that waiver impliedly, by referring to privileged documents or conversations in interlocutory proceedings, points of claim or other correspondence.

In practice parties to litigation are compelled to disclose privileged material.

Public interest privilege

An arbitrator must not under any circumstances order a person to disclose information which it would be contrary to the public interest to force him to reveal. Similarly he must not allow a party to put in evidence information which is covered by such "*public interest immunity*"

Claimants to immunity

The usual claimant to public immunity privilege will be a government department or other limb or the Crown. In very limited circumstances, however, a non-governmental agency may be able to establish the immunity.

Proof of relevancy

The party seeing to obtain or to use the information for which the immunity is claimed must first show that the information is likely to be relevant to some question in the arbitration:

Proof of a public interest

No immunity attaches on the mere ground that the information sought was given or received in confidence. Some public interest in preserving its secrecy must be found: the arbitrator ought not to accept a claim to immunity based upon purely private grounds:

Once relevancy and a recognized public interest are shown, the tribunal proceeds to balance the public interests described. This involves a deal of discretion

The tribunal is not allowed to inspect the thing for which the privilege is claimed unless and until it concludes, having heard argument upon the balance of interests, that the scales are evenly balanced.

Journalistic sources:
Journalists and their associated staff have a special, statutory, immunity from compulsion to reveal the source of information which has been supplied to them in confidence and which they have used in a publication or broadcast:

> In the course of arbitration proceedings, no person can usually be compelled to produce any document or to answer any questions if such document or answer any question if such document or answer would have a tendency to expose him to a real risk of prosecution for an offence under the law of England and Wales. This is the common law privilege against self-incrimination. And is connected with the general right of silence which suspects possess in criminal cases. It is the English equivalent of the United States' Fifth Amendment.

The arbitrator is probably under no duty to remind the witness that he may be entitled to the privilege, though it is sensible to have a reminder when it is fairly clear that the witness may incriminate himself or his spouse by giving the evidence requested of him.

It is wise to entitle "without prejudice" a letter or conversation which is a genuine attempt to settle a dispute, but the absence of that title will not necessarily be fatal to the communication's being protected by the privilege:

The privilege will however be denied to a letter which contains a "without prejudice" title if, on closer examination by the court, it proves to be not part of a genuine attempt to settle an existing dispute:

Whether or not without prejudice communications lead to a settlement of the dispute, the contents of those communications cannot be ordered disclosed to persons who were not involved in their making or receipt, and cannot be used in evidence by such persons, without the consent of all the parties to them:

If without prejudice communications lead to a settlement of the dispute, they become admissible *in evidence between the parties to them for the purpose of establishing the existence and terms of the settlement, and for enforcing it through the courts. If however the communications prove fruitless and the dispute proceeds to trail, they are admissible, if at all, only on the question of costs at the conclusion of the judgment.*

WORDS OF WISDOM

"Grant that I may not so much seek
To be consoled as to console
To be understood as to understand
To be loved as to love
For it is in giving that we receive
It is in pardoning that we are
pardoned
It is in injury to self that we are
born
To eternal life-" Wayne Dyer

"Some individuals see the world
as merciless and uncaring
while others see it as wise and
compassionate, and they have
different experiences as a
result"—Gary Zukav

CHAPTER 10

HEARING OF THE CASE - THE BIG DAY, DEPENDING ON WHAT COLOUR LENS YOU SEE THIS

This chapter will give some useful pointers as to how to take part in this process. You do not have to be a "Perry Mason' to successfully play this game. Here as some 'dos' and don'ts '

Opening addresses

They are made in such hearings and there is value in setting the scene to put the legal and factual issues in context. There is no standard format.

Things to avoid:

a) Overstatement

This is not the time to try to 'sell your case". Rather, assist and inform the tribunal about your case. Moderation is the key.

b) Avoid too much detail

This is not the time to present your evidence. It is a map of your case where you introduce your story and cast of witnesses so the tribunal should know who you are calling, when and why.

The tribunal has your trial agenda and knows what to expect and what to expect as the evidence unfolds.

c) Argument

This is not the place for argument, which should be left for closing. You are only setting the case for the tribunal.

This is also not the time to anticipate defences therefore DO:

- Provide a broad context
- What is the trial about?
- What is your theory of the case?
- Without using legalese tell them why your client is in court.
- Give a factual and legal context in which to consider the evidence.
- Introduce the parties
- State the cause of action
- State the facts
- Direct the tribunal to particular points (eg "She was the only person not drinking at the party")

- Use exhibits in your opening, even a clause in a contract
- Have a prepared legal brief on the law or an outline of the legal issues with copies of the leading cases
- You can refer to defences raised and defuse key weaknesses in your case and on which the defendant will rely
- Outline the relief sought. Tie the quantum of damages to the facts and evidence that will be presented

End with:

"That concludes the opening and with the leave of this tribunal I would now like to call my first witness"

DEFENDANTS OPENING:
- Should be short and to the point
- No need to review the cause of action, the facts of the case or the law
- Rather, concentrate on a few legal or factual issues, and clarify the defendant's position thereon.
- Then, highlight and outline the details of witnesses as in the case of the plaintiff

Therefore outline of the "who, what and when" of the case and save the attacks for closing

- Story telling is a powerful tool.
- Be succinct and helpful

CLOSING ARGUMENTS
- 80%-90 % of the closing arguments should have been prepared before the trial starts (cases to rely on, organisation of the argument, and evidence in support of arguments).
- The last 10% can be on evidence adduced which can never be predicted accurately.
- A book of case authorities is prepared, properly bound and tabbed with highlighting.
- Copies for each tribunal member and for opposing counsel.

Things to AVOID IN CLOSINGS:
- Do not misstate the evidence
- Inform the tribunal of all pertinent authority
- Do not refer to facts not in evidence
- Do not use impassioned rhetoric ("reason" rather)
- Do not state your beliefs, let the facts and the law speak for them

- Avoid personal attacks

THEREFORE;
- A good closing meshes the facts, the law and policy.
- Be flexible so as to fit the argument to the case as long as there is a structure

For example:
Opening paragraph
- Statements of the points in issue

Issue 1: Review applicable community/society evidence and law relating thereto
Conclusion (strongest first)

"That concludes my submission on the first issue"
- Convince tribunal that your interpretation is more compelling
- Highlight particular, important evidence
- Resolve disputes presented by evidence
- Cite corroboration and consistency
- Cite inconsistencies, bias contradictions and look for confirmations of your case
- Expand on undisputed facts. Concentrate on credibility
- Use visual aids where possible
- Present a crisp convincing case.
- Blend all pieces together

- Present your argument before attacking the other side's position and exhibits
- Explain the law and apply it to the facts to distinguish a case on the facts or challenge it on the law
- Keep it short.
- Integrate the quoted proposition with facts of this case and show direct application
- This is not a story—state position at beginning of argument without narrating the whole case
- Use direct quotes

RIGHT OF REPLY:
- Last word is important
- Capture theme in a short strong statement
- Do not respond to a whole list of minor errors
- Deal with major misstatements of the law or facts

WORDS OF WISDOM

"I know that the very essence of my being be the way of transforming my life is love" - Wayne Dyer

CHAPTER 11

EXAMINATION AND CROSS EXAMINATION (X)

After preliminary issues have been deal with and after opening statements the parties actually present their evidence the usual order being:

i.   The evidence of the party who initiated the proceedings
ii. Evidence of any other parties with a similar interest in the outcome
iii. Evidence of the opposing parties
iv. Includes questioning of witnesses by the parties or their reps

The examination-in-chief
The witness may be questioned by other parties whose interest or position is similar. In the exam in chief parties are expected to ask 'open questions' ie invite the witness to provide an independent response. It does not suggest the answer that the questioner is looking for nor does it contain crucial facts or conclusions that the questioner wants the witness to confirm. It does not put words in the witness's mouth.
Leading questions are allowed only in non-controversial matters like undisputed background facts or points where the witness needs clarification. Then the X takes place

The importance of the cross examination (X) is overrated. Preparation involves gathering info about the opposing witness and their evidence. So the prep aims at structuring the X so as to get info from the witness that you need disclosed and not info that you don't want to have raised. Control of the process is crucial: you determine the agenda and you ask the questions.

PURPOSE of the Cross Examination (X):
1. To discredit the testimony of the said witness
2. To discredit the unfavourable testimony of other witnesses
3. To corroborate favourable testimony of other witnesses
4. To contribute independently to the favourable dev of your own case.

Others say
1. To bring forth favourable testimony from the witness AND discredit unfavourable testimony from the said witness

The aim is not to" destroy "the witness
They can get angry but you should be polite, sincere and with integrity. Therefore follow the help me out approach

Know your goals

Why has the witness been called?

How will he help their case?

How can he hurt your case?

Based on this info you can select areas for the X

Know the evidence. E.g. from the discovery process and documents, witness statements. There is no obligation to speak.

(With leave) you may examine for discovery the witness. You can order the production of relevant documents.

Have a witness be present during discovery.

At the hearing, listen carefully to each witness.

New avenues may reveal themselves.

Visit the scene.

2. Know yourself.

Don't appear fake.

8. Why the X

It is not a "must". If he has not hurt your case do not X

But it is necessary to challenge contradictory evidence.

So present this contradictory evidence (Rule in Browning v. Dunn)

PRINCIPLES

1. Be brief

2. Keep it short (one line per question)

It is difficult to evade a simple, direct question

3. Don't use leading questions
4. Know when to stop (once they have been discredited, stop)
5. Do not quarrel with the witness
6. Plan your questions. Be subtle and indirect
7. Listen carefully to the witness
   Has the question been answered? If not, ask again.
   Silent spells during submissions allow issues to be digested by the audience
8. Start safe and finish strong.
   Start in a safe area (where you know what the answers s/b. Avoid negative last impressions.
9. Ask not only the right question but ask it the right way.
10. Putting it all together.
    You tell the witness the facts you want. Cross refer the facts to them. Then should the witness deny a fact you can impeach the witness.

Re-examination:
After X, the party who called the witness may ask him further questions to clarify answers he provided or address new issues that arose in the X
Other parties may ask further questions.

ALWAYS REMEMBER TO KISS (KEEP IT SHORT AND SIMPLE)!!

WORDS OF WISDOM

"Dignity does not consist in processing honours but in deserving them" - Aristotle

Grounds for objection

Info sought is irrelevant, unreliable, unnecessary or unfair

Questions repetitive or "bullying" in nature

Answer unreliable (i.e. based on hearsay or speculation

Answer outside witness's knowledge (ordinary witness asked an expert opinion

Opinions outside his area of expertise

Asking leading questions

WORDS OF WISDOM

Broken dreams
"As children bring their broken toys
With tears to mend,
I brought my broken dreams to
God - Because he was my friend
But instead of leaving him to do
the mending, I hung around and
tried to interfere with ways that were
my own
At last I stretched them back and
cried "how can you be so slow?"
"My child" he said "what could I
do - you never let them go"

Unknown author

CHAPTER 12

THE AWARD - WHO GETS WHAT AND WHY

An understanding of the rules on awards can go a long way to ensuring that the award is proper and has properly been arrived at.

The 7 C's of an award:

1. Clear and Certain
2. Concise
3. Comprehensive
4. Competent
5. Consistent
6. Conclusive
7. Capable of Performance.

General Rules:

- Unless the parties otherwise agree, the decision of the majority of the members of a tribunal is the tribunal's award. If there is no majority, the decision of the chair is the award.
- Unless the parties agree otherwise, the dispute must be decided in accordance with the law and the arbitration agreement, the contract under which the dispute arose and any applicable usages of trade.
- Unless the parties otherwise agree, an award must be made in writing and must state the reasons it is based upon.

- Unless the parties otherwise agree, the arbitrators can, in addition to damages, award:

  i. Specific performance, injunctions and other equitable remedies.

  ii. The cost of the arbitration.

  iii. Pre award interest (in the same way as courts grant pre-judgement interest.

  iv. Arbitrators have no power to award punitive or exemplary damages.

WORDS OF WISDOM

"My judgements prevent me from seeing the good that lies beyond appearances" - *Wayne Dyer*

THE ARBITRATORS DISCRETION AS TO COSTS

Unless the arbitration agreement otherwise provides the cost of the award and of the reference are within the discretion of the arbitrator who may direct by and to whom and in what manner these cost or any parts of them should be paid the practice of the high court cost follow the event i.e. that in the ordinary way the successful party should receive his costs thus if without giving good reasons arbiter awards that the cost shall been borne in the same whether questions in a special case or answered in favour of one partite or the other that shows sufficiently . . . that he is excluding from his mind in the arriving at his order what ought to be the most important consideration effecting it and he is guilty of technical miss conducts so that the part of the award may be set aside.

The arbitrator should not depart from the rule that costs follow the event without the substantial reasons and he should always bear in mind the duty to act judicially by excluding of his mind and matter not strictly connected with abruption.

Where the award is final the court will not compel the arbitrator to give reasons instead it treats an award depriving a successful party of all or part of the costs without stating any reason as prima facie evidence of misconduct and on any application to set aside or remit the award of cost on the grounds of such misconduct.

WORDS OF WISDOM

"The greatest human quest is to know what one must do in order to become a human being" - Immanuel Kant

CHAPTER 13

CHALLENGES TO THE AWARD . . . . BACK TO SQUARE 1?!

The courts will not interfere unless an injustice has been done. So what kind of injustice?
Over the years in most common law jurisdictions the courts are more and more reluctant to interfere in the arbitrate in process, except to prevent real injustice
There is a difference between setting aside an award and having an award remitted on various grounds. There are generally 6 specific grounds for remitting an award to an arbitrator to reconsider the case:

i.   where the award is ambiguous or uncertain or inconsistent with the arbitration clause in the original contract providing for the award
ii.   Where the arbitrator has made a mistake and he/she has made a request for it to be remitted to him, for example to comply with the arbitration agreement, mistakenly awarded payment to the wrong person or a mistake as to the principle on which the award is based
iii. There has been 'misconduct on the part of the arbitrator'

iv. Material evidence which could not be obtained earlier with reasonable diligence has surfaced

v. Where an arbitrator requests the court for a' question of Law" or "special case", and insufficient info has been provided by the said arbitrator

vi. where there has been a" misunderstanding" causing injustice (although no "misconduct" by the arbitrator).

vii. Where there has been non-compliance with legal requirements be they on procedural matters, or a significant matter in relation to the agreement between the parties.

viii. where the arbitrator has misconducted himself and/or the proceedings. This may include proceedings ex parte (without sufficient cause, where the arbitrator is excluding persons without sufficient cause, improperly receiving evidence or where there improper delegation of duties, by the said arbitrator.

CHAPTER 14

. . . NEVER HAVING TO SAY YOUR'E SORRY'

I am reminded of the above phrase, made popular in the movie 'love Story'
It is ironic that in a potential dispute you never say 'sorry' or you are liable to the other party in damages!

I quote the following, which could not have been presented more succinctly.

The power of an apology From "Conflict Resolution Today"
March 2006
"A conversation between Evita Roche and Neil Sargent"

Many professionals are advised not to apologize when they make a mistake. However according to researcher Jonathan Cohen from University of Florida approximately 30 percent of plaintiffs in medical malpractice suits claim they wouldn't have sued if only there had been an apology.
Do we dare to apologize when we are genuinely sorry? Evita Roche and Neil Sargent, two lawyers, academics and mediators explore this question.

Neil: What is apology that is so important to you?

Evita: I believe most disputes are fundamentally
         about hurt feelings and, unless these are
         talked about and repaired, the dispute
         won't be "fixed" in any real, stable way.
         Apologies can be a big part of restoring a
         relationship. Apologies can help resolve "big
         table" conflicts as well, like commercial,
         workplace, and health care disputes. And
         on the international stage, we've seen how
         important apologies can be, what with the
         number of countries seeking them, and the
         time and energy many politicians spend
         avoiding them.

Neil: It seems to me that by avoiding the simple
         act of an apology, we allow disputes to
         become so much more complicated than
         they need to be.

Evita: Yes, I think we spend enormous
         resources - time, money and
         energy - avoiding the simple fact that
         a meaningful apology can stop a lot of
         disputes from escalating

Neil: So should apologies be part of a good
         settlement package?

Evita: Yes, as long as the apology is genuine and not offered just to avoid the substantive parts of a settlement package, like money or other remedies. The apology breaks the ice and lets the parties reconnect, making it possible for them to move forward and talk about what a fair settlement would look like.

Neil: What is it about an apology that can satisfy some of the deepest needs of a person or group?

Evita: Apologies satisfy a deep need to be heard, understood and listened to non-judgementally. A conflict resolution organization I once worked with had T-shirts that said, "Just talk to me." I think that deep down; people do want to talk with each other. They may need help to do so, at least initially, but this is what they want, this is what they find satisfying. Lawsuits make us feel more powerful, at least temporarily, but they don't usually satisfy deep human needs. The law deals with rights and obligations. It's like Einstein said, problems can't be fixed at the same level as they were created. Apologies, it seems, are simply a good business practice.

We're seeking this lot in the U.S. now, particularly in the health care field, where HMO's are doing everything they can to reduce the cost of medical malpractice disputes. They're pushing for ways to allow physicians to apologise for mistakes without having to fear they will be sued. If an apology can bee seen as an admission of liability, the answer is to change the law.

Neil: There are signs that things are getting better. As you know, several U.S. states and I think all of the Australian states have passed some kind of apology legislation. So that expression of sympathy and other regret and other "benevolent gestures", as they call them, are not admissible in evidence.

CHAPTER 15

SOME ADMINISTRATIVE LAW SALAD TO DIGEST

FUNDAMENTAL PRINCIPLES OF ADMINISTRATIVE LAW APPLICABLE TO TRIBUNALS AND ARBITRATION PANELS

Must stay within their jurisdiction

ii. Must exercise their judgment in a reasonable manner

PROCEDURAL FAIRNESS

The concept of procedural fairness requires that;

1. The rules of natural Justice must be followed
2. Notice must be given of the intended decision
3. Right to an impartial decision maker
4. The rule against sub-delegation
5. Natural Justice
    i.   Right to be heard
    ii. Requirements to act within jurisdiction
    iii. Powers limited to those established by law and must follow procedures set out therein. AND to do everything that the tribunal is required to do within a reasonable time
6. Requirements as to Discretion.
    a. Where granted must apply legislation to each situation.

b. Considerations of policy and public interest should be taken into account.

c. Discretion must be exercised in a fair and reasonable manner.

d. Must be based on intent and purpose of enabling law/ rules and not personal beliefs or values.

e. Must only consider relevant factors

f. Similar cases s/b treated in a similar way

g. Must be exercised in good faith

h. Discretion must not be fettered so rule out irrelevant or inappropriate options otherwise fettering

i. Where power granted cannot refuse to exercise that discretion and cannot refuse to consider relevant factors

j. "Discretion must still be exercised within a reasonable interpretation of the k. margin of manoeuvre contemplated by the law, principles of admin law governing the exercise of discretion and consistent with the Canadian Charter of Rights and Freedoms (Baker v. Canada)

Ways to minimise uncertainty without fettering discretion:

a. Consult policy guidelines, rules

b. Consult with others as long as tribunal makes final decision and consultation voluntarily, and no pressure to make a particular decision and no new factors/issues without prior notice and permission of parties.

4th principle.
THE RULE AGAINST SUB-DELEGATION
Delegatus non protest delegare (Latin for "A delegate cannot delegate"). This is to preserve quality and ensure fairness of decisions.

WHERE PROCEDURAL FAIRNESS RULES ARE FOUND
- The nature of the decision (is it administrative/ quasi judicial?)
- The nature of the statutory scheme
- The importance of the decision, to he affected party
- Legitimate expectation of a particular process
- Intention of legislature of tribunal to choose its own procedure

Statutory fairness requirements take precedence over common law requirements

TWO COMMON LAW PRINCIPLES

1. The right to be heard
2. The right to an unbiased decision maker

1. THE RIGHT TO BE HEARD. (No single formula)

SPPA (On) requirements for tribunals affected more stringent

I.e. requirements for oral hearing where all parties physically present

X to be permitted.

Amendment in 1990's written and electronic hearings allowed without consent as long as no prejudice to anyone.

Interrogatories allowed in lieu of X.

Notice of proceedings

a. With sufficient explanation to address issues

b. Sufficient time to prepare

Limits on such rights:

On court of appeal held that tribunal cannot compel parties to disclose evidence in advance unless statute empowers it or procedural fairness rules require this On Human Rights Commission v. Dofasco Inc.

- Right to be present throughout hearing
- And tribunal members may not discuss with one party alone.
  (In written hearings each party gets relevant information with the right to respond)
- In electronic hearings each party is to hear each other and tribunal.

All parties must be able to see video conference.

Limits on right to be present:
a. If party served with notice and does not attend
b. Where party disrupting proceedings
c. If party "walks out"
d. Sensitivity of evidence and one party blabbermouth

Right to be represented:
- Question clients own witnesses X raise objections to procedure or admissibility of evidence and make submissions.
- Limits
- Incompetent non-witness
- Non compliance with duties and responsibilities of advocate or adviser
- No absolute right to adjournment to obtain representation

NB: Advise parties early on such rights, intention of parties to be represented, time needed to find representation and efforts to be made
Parties not always entitled to 1st rep choice
Right to present evidence
To establish facts
Mechanism should be in place to allow the third party to provide info to a party

Limits to such rights

No right to present it ORALLY

Not if against rules of procedure or if irrelevant or unreliable

RIGHT TO X

Party must know evidence and to respond thereto. Must be in good time and not irrelevant or unreliable.

(Includes written info)

X must not be inflammatory abusive or repetitive SPPA and APA of BC provide reasonable rights to control procedures in this context.

2. THE RIGHT TO AN UNBIASED DECISION MAKER.

IMPARTIALTY (2nd PILLAR OF PROCEDURAL FAIRNESS)

(1st pillar right to be heard—as summarised above)

HE WHO HEARS MUST DECIDE IN AN UNFETTERED MANNER EXCEPTION: prolonged illness or death, remaining members can render the decision. But some statutes require interest group to be present eg Union/Management.

Can make collegial decision making (of peers etc.). But the decision must be unfettered.

Decision must be based on submissions presented but entitled to "take notice" or "administrative notice" of well informed community member or professional group.

THE REQUIREMENTS TO GIVE REASONED DECISIONS

Generally required where an individual's rights, privileges, interests affected or to be able to appeal All relevant Acts require it but in on where parties require reasons.

Test

- Was there a reasonable apprehension of bias? (Must be a reasonable one held by reasonable and right right-minded persons applying themselves to the question and obtaining thereon the required information).
- Tribunal well informed, right-minded, practical and realistic. Relevant circumstances including the traditions of integrity and impartiality.
- There is a strong presumption of judicial integrity that can only be displaced by cogent contrary evidence
- Conflict of interest (e.g. financial or other interest) only one source of perceived bias

INDICATORS OF BIAS:
- Meets with one party alone
- Close friendship/ relationship with 1 party
- Financial interest or association member
- Expresses opinion
- Intervenes in favour of one party or expresses a dislike
- Party to litigation against a party or witness
- Past bus or professional association
- Receives a gift

ELEMENTS OF INSTITUTIONAL BIAS:
Whilst individual= state of mind. Tribunal = status.
Executive, legislative, business or corporate interests or other pressure groups.
Duty of impartiality is not the same as duty to be independent.
Degree of Independence one factor re impartiality or institutional bias

Factors to gauge Institutional bias:
- Closeness in relationship with govt dept
- Multiple functions with overlap by employees

Factors to gauge independence from govt:
i.   Appointment "at pleasure" or fixed term
ii. If fixed term, how long?
iii. Fixed salary (ok) or at will of govt

iv.   Part time or full time (ok)
v.   Discretion of chair to appoint panel (not ok)
vi.   Employees appointed by govt (not ok)
vii. Requirement of tribunal to follow govt policy?
      (not ok)
viii. Minister evaluates chair? (not ok)
ix.   Govt. Funding? (not ok)

Must be clear separation - investigating and admin action.
Argue case and admin decision.

EXCEPTION Re inst bias
If statute requires above negative factors

Allegation of bias should be made ASAP.

CHAPTER 16

SOME CANADIAN STATUTE LAW GOVERNING ARBITRATION TRIBUNALS - JUST SALAD DRESSING

I have endeavoured to summarise in a fashion as lucid as possible, some statutory provisions in Canada governing arbitrations in 3 of the more populous provinces—but the arbitrator will be aware of this—or should be. It is worthwhile knowing some of these provisions.

Ontario (Statutory Powers Procedure Act—SPPA)
Alberta (Admin Procedures Act)
B.C (Admin. Tribunals Act)

	ON (SPPA)	AB (APA)	BC(ATA)
APPLICATION	Not gov't officials (hospitals, universities, professional clubs, churches)	Tribunals + 7 named agencies when statutory decision affecting rights. Less stringent and formal then ON hospitals, varsities, clubs, churches	ATA no govt officers. Only tribunals where expressly provided

92

HEARINGS	Oral unless other form justified. Since 1990 written and electronic allowed without consent (but no prejudice)	Must be oral. If written inadequate. Therefore oral right not inherent	
NOTICE OF HEARINGS	To indicate stat. authority, purpose, format of hearing	Must be given 510 minister can establish dealings	
DECISIONS		S3 must provide notice of intention	
RELEVANT EVIDENCE	Must provide	Must provide	Must provide
X	Must permit (interrogatories allowed)	Must permit (where info adverse and not contradicted)	
OATH	Optional	Optional	Optional
INADMISSABLE EVIDENCE	OK	OK	OK
LEGAL REPRESENTATIVE	Right given	No right	Right given
AWARDS		Written reasoned awards required	Written reasoned awards required

STATEMENT OF FACT	Only by request otherwise not required	Required	
AUTHORITY TO MAKE RULES Witness summons Disclosure of evidence Prehearing conference Error corrections in awards Enforcement Appeal provisions power to control process	Yes	Silent	Yes
DISCLOSURE OF EVIDENCE	Tribunal cannot compel in advance unless statute empowers or procedural fairness rules require them DEFASCO		
CONTROL Re: inflammatory, abusive or repetitive	Reasonable rights	Reasonable rights	Reasonable rights

The various stages are as follows

1 Fixing the procedure. The arbitrator and the parties satisfy themselves that there are no misunderstandings as to the general nature of the procedure to be adopted. The arbitrator also gives any detailed directions which are required.

2 Defining the issues. The parties, helped if necessary by the arbitrator, identify the issues of fact and law on which the arbitrator will be required to reach a decision when making his award.

3 Production and preparation of the documents. Relevant documents are disclosed and inspected by the parties, and are prepared for the hearing.

4 Interim protection orders. The arbitrator or the Court makes orders relating to any property which is either the subject matter of the dispute, or is the subject of an issue in the reference. The purpose of such orders may be to protect the property itself from harm; to preserve the rights of the parties until the dispute has been resolved; or to enable the parties to exploit the evidentiary value of the property to the full.

5 Orders for security. The arbitrator or the Court makes orders securing the right of the party who is ultimately successful to recover his costs

of the arbitration; and securing the right of a successful claimant to be paid the amount of the award.

6 Arranging the hearing. If the arbitration is of a type which calls for an oral hearing, a date and place are appointed.

7 Investigation of facts and law; the hearing. If the arbitration is of a type which calls for an oral hearing, the parties and their representatives and witnesses appear before the arbitrator to present their case on the facts and the law. If the procedure does not involve a hearing, the same investigation takes place, but in an informal and abbreviated manner.

8 The decision. The arbitrator reaches his decision in the light of the evidence and arguments brought before him, and also in the light of any advice from third persons which it is permissible for him to obtain.

9 The award. The arbitrator embodies his decision in an award, which he then publishes.

10 Appeal proceedings. Where the contract so provides, an appellate arbitral tribunal reconsiders the decision of the arbitrator.

APPENDIX 1

SAMPLE ARBITRATION AGREEMENT

This AGREEMENT made the _____day
of_____20

BETWEEN:

AND

WHEREAS, the parties entered into an
Agreement dated_____(hereinafter called the
"Agreement");

AND WHEREAS, the parties wish to refer a
certain dispute arising under the Agreement to
arbitration, which dispute is more fully defined
below, and to settle certain procedural matters
related to the arbitration;

AND, no party is under any duress or undue
influence of the other and are voluntarily
entering into this Agreement.

NOW THEREFORE, in order that the said dispute be finally settled and determined, it is hereby agreed that the dispute be submitted for arbitration, as follows:

DEFINITION OF DISPUTE TO BE ARBITRATED

PLACE OF ARBITRATION

JURISDICTION AND ARBITRATION RULES

The parties acknowledge and agree that the Arbitrator is properly constituted in accordance with this Agreement and has jurisdiction to hear and determine the dispute hereby submitted to arbitration.

EXISTING LEGAL ACTION

All existing legal actions shall not be discontinued during the process of this Arbitration but all proceedings shall be stayed until an Award is published.

AGREEMENT BINDING

This Agreement shall be binding upon the heirs, executors, administrators and assigns of the parties hereto

RULES OF EVIDENCE

The Arbitrator shall apply the principles of natural justice and shall not be bound by the strict rules of evidence in force in the courts of this Province, but may receive any evidence submitted to it by the parties that the Arbitrator believes to be relevant to the matters in controversy, or that will enable the Arbitrator to arrive at a fair and proper decision. The arbitrator shall have full power and authority to rule on any questions of law applying to the admission of evidence or determination of the issues.

DEFAULT

PERIOD FOR THE AWARD

The Arbitrator shall communicate his award to the parties not later than thirty (30) days after the close of the hearings, subject to any reasonable delay due to unforeseen circumstances.

CONFIDENTIALTY

The arbitration proceedings are strictly confidential. No portion of the evidence, or the Award, shall be disclosed to anyone other than an authorized representative of the parties except;

A. By a party with the written consent of the other party;

B. By the Arbitrator with the written consent of both parties.

IN WITNESS WHEREOF the parties have duly executed this Agreement as of the day and year first above written.

APPENDIX 2

ARBITRATION PANEL MEMBER'S NOTES

Chairperson of Panel _____

Member_____

Member_____

Person writing_____

ISSUES THE PANEL WAS ASKED TO DECIDE

FINDINGS OF FACT THAT RELATES TO THE ISSUES

SUMMARY OF APPLICANT'S POSITION

SUMMARY OF RESPONDENT'S POSITION.

NOTE TO PANEL MEMBERS *please ensure that all panel member's Notes along with one copy of all Exhibits is attached for retention*

APPENDIX 3

MEDIATION/ ARBITRATION AGREEMENT (COMBINATION)

This AGREEMENT made the _____day of_____20

BETWEEN:

AND

WHEREAS, the parties entered into an Agreement dated_____(hereinafter called the "Agreement");

AND WHEREAS, the parties wish to refer a certain dispute arising under the Agreement to mediation and arbitration, which dispute is more fully defined below, and to settle certain procedural matters related to the arbitration;

AND WHEREAS, no party is under any duress or undue influence of the other, and are voluntarily entering into this Agreement.

NOW THEREFORE, in order that the said dispute be finally settled and determined, it is hereby agreed that the dispute be submitted for arbitration, as follows:

DEFINITION OF DISPUTE TO BE ARBITRATED

PLACE OF ARBITRATION

JURISDICTION AND ARBITRATION RULES
The parties acknowledge and agree that the Arbitrator is properly constituted in accordance with this Agreement and has jurisdiction to hear and determine the dispute hereby submitted to arbitration.

EXISTING LEGAL ACTION
All existing legal actions shall not be discontinued during the process of this

Arbitration but all proceedings shall be stayed until an Award is published.

AGREEMENT BINDING

This Agreement shall be binding upon the heirs, executors, administrators and assigns of the parties hereto.

RULES OF EVIDENCE

The Arbitrator shall apply the principles of natural justice and shall not be bound by the strict rules of evidence in force in the courts of this Province, but may receive any evidence submitted to it by the parties that the Arbitrator believes to be relevant to the matters in controversy or that will enable the Arbitrator to arrive at a fair and proper decision. The arbitrator shall have full power and authority to rule on any questions of law applying to the admission of evidence or determination of the issues.

DEFAULT

PERIOD FOR THE AWARD

The Arbitrator shall communicate his award to the parties not later than thirty (30) days after the close of the hearings, subject to any reasonable delay due to unforeseen circumstances.

CONFIDENTIALTY

The arbitration proceedings are strictly confidential. No portion of the evidence, or the Award, shall be disclosed to anyone other than an authorized representative of the parties except

A. By a party with the written consent of the other party;

B. By the Arbitrator with the written consent of both parties.

IN WITNESS WHEREOF the parties have duly executed this Agreement as of the day and year first above written.

APPENDIX 4

Short form procedure RULES

1. Adoption of the short form Procedure

1.1 - The parties may agree at any time prior to or during the course of the arbitration to adopt this short form procedure, and in that event the Rules set out there from shall be modified as hereafter provided;

2.1 - The arbitration will be conducted on a documents only basis subject to the discretion of the arbitrator to order a meeting for clarification purposes of no more than one day in length in respect of the whole or any part of the arbitration.

2.2 - Unless the Arbitrator otherwise directs the arbitration will proceed on the basis of exchange of Statements of Case as hereinafter set out;

2.3 - All statements of case shall contain the following:
   a. A full statement of the party's arguments of fact and law;
   b. A signed and dated statement of the evidence of any witness upon whose evidence the party relies;

c. Copies of all documents the contents of which the party relies on;
d. A full statement of the remedies claimed;
e. Detailed calculations of any sums claimed;

2.4 - Unless the arbitrator otherwise directs the parties will exchange Statements of Case as follows;

a. Within 28 days of the receipt by the Claimant of the Arbitrator's acceptance of the appointment the claimant shall send to the arbitrator and to the other party his statement of claim

b. The respondent shall within 28 days from receipt of the statement of Claim send to the Arbitrator and the Claimant a Statement of Defence. If no Statement of defence is served within that time limit or such extended time limit as the Arbitrator may allow then the Respondent will be debarred from serving a Statement of Defence;

c. If the Respondent wishes to make any counterclaim then his Statement of Case shall include that counterclaim.

d. The claimant shall within 14 days from receipt of Defence and within 28 days from receipt of the statement of counterclaim, (if any) send to the Arbitrator and to the other Party a Reply and Defence to Counterclaim (if any).If no statement of defence to counterclaim is served within that time limit or such extended time limit as the Arbitrator may allow then the claimant will be debarred from serving a Defence to Counterclaim

e. The respondent shall within 14 days from receipt of the Defence to Counterclaim send to the arbitrator and to the other Party a reply to Defence to counterclaim;

f. Any further statements may only be served with the leave of the Arbitrator;

g. When a Respondent or Claimant has been debarred from serving a Defence or Defence to counterclaim or (t0 above the other party or parties) will be required to prove any allegations made in his or their Statements of Case.

2.5 - Before or after close of exchanges of Statements of Case the arbitrator may give detailed directions with any appropriate timetable for all further procedural steps in the arbitration, including (but not limited to) the following:

a. Any amendment to, expansion of, summary of, or reproduction in some other format of, any Statement of Case or any extension to or alteration of time limits for service of Statements of Case.

b. Disclosure and production of documents as between the parties;

c. The exchange of statements of evidence of witnesses of fact;

d. The number and types of experts and exchange of their reports;

e. Meeting between experts;

f. Arrangements for any oral hearing if, in the exercise of his discretion, he concludes that any oral hearing is necessary including any time limits to be imposed on the length of oral submissions or the examination or cross examination of witnesses.

2.6 - The arbitrator may at any time order any of the following to be delivered to him in writing;

a. Submissions to be advanced by or on behalf of any party;

- Questions intended to be put to any witness.

- Answers by any witness to identified questions.

3. Rules of Evidence

3.1- In any arbitration under the Short Form Procedure, the parties are deemed to have waived all rules and requirements in respect of the law relating to admissibility of evidence, unless at any stage before publication of any award (whether or not the final or last award), any party notifies the arbitrator in writing of that party's wish to withdraw such waiver.

3.2- In any event withdrawal of such waiver shall not take effect unless the arbitrator in his absolute discretion consents thereto.

3.3- Before consenting to withdrawal of such waiver, the arbitrator shall permit the other party or parties to make such representation, whether orally or in wring, as he considers appropriate.

3.4- In the event of such withdrawal taking effect, the arbitrator shall give such directions, either in writing or by way of holding a preliminary meeting for the further conduct of the arbitration as he considers appropriate, and may take into account the fact of the withdrawal of such waiver in considering the exercise of his discretion to ward costs.

Where any agreement, submission or reference provides for arbitration under the XYZ COMMUNITY/SOCIETY Scheme, (the scheme), the Parties shall have taken to have agreed that the arbitration shall be conducted in accordance with theses Rules, or any modified, amended or substituted Rules which have come into effect before the commencement of that arbitration.

APPENDIX 5

SAMPLE COMMUNITY ARBITRATION RULES

1. INTRODUCTORY

1.1- These Rules are intended to be dealt with in conjunction with the Arbitration Legislation currently in force in Alberta and incorporate all provisions of the legislation, except for any provision that is not mandatory and is expressly modified by these Rules or by the agreement of the Parties.

1.2- These Rules are Institutional Rules for the purposes of S- of the Act.

1.3- The parties may not amend or modify these Rules or any procedure under them after the appointment of an Arbitrator, unless the Arbitrator agrees to such amendment or modification.

1.4- All expressions used in these Rules, which are also used in the Act, have the same meaning as they do in the Act.

2. COMMENCEMENT OF THE ARBITRATION.

2.1- The arbitration shall be regarded as commenced in accordance with the provisions of S 23 of the Act.

2.2- Any Party wishing to commence an arbitration under these Rules (the Claimant) shall serve on the XYZ COMMUNITY/SOCIETY, using the prescribed form (the Arbitration Notice) with a copy to the other Party, a written request for arbitration under these rules accompanied by:

   a. The names, addresses, telephone and fax numbers and e-mail addresses of the Parties to the arbitration.
   b. Copies of the Contractual documents (if any) in which the arbitration agreement is contained or under which the arbitration arises, or an agreement signed by all the parties that the matter(s) in dispute should be referred to arbitration under these rules.
   c. A brief statement describing the nature and circumstances of the dispute and specifying the relief claimed.

3.   APPOINTING AUTHORITY/APPOINTMENT OF THE ARBITRATOR

3.1- The appointing Authority under these rules will be the XYZ COMMUNITY/SOCIETY

3.2- UPON RECEIPT OF THE Arbitration Notice on the prescribed form, the XYZ COMMUNITY/SOCIETY will appoint a suitable Arbitrator having due regard to any agreement between the Parties as to the qualifications required of the Arbitrator.

3.3- Upon receipt of the Arbitration Notice on the prescribed form, the Institute will also expect to have received from the Claimant the following:

a. The names and addresses of all the Parties to the arbitration;

b. A brief statement of the nature and circumstances of the dispute(s).

c. A copy of the arbitration clause in the Contract or agreement signed by all the Parties that the dispute (so should be referred to arbitration);

d. Confirmation that any conditions precedent have been complied with, and any other relevant document.

3.4- If the arbitrator dies or is unable to, or refuses, to act, the XYZ COMMUNITY/SOCIETY will appoint another Arbitrator on the application of any of the Parties.

4. COMMUNICATIONS BETWEEN PARTIES AND THE ARBITRATOR

4.1- When the Arbitrator sends any communication to one party, he shall send a copy to the other Party or Parties.

4.2- Any communication sent by a Party to the XYZ COMMUNITY/SOCIETY prior to the Arbitrator's Appointment, or to the Arbitrator once appointed, shall be copied by that Party to the other Party or Parties and marked as having as having been so copied.

4.3- The address of a Party or their representatives, for the purpose of communications during the course of the proceedings, shall be as most recently notified to the Arbitrator and the other Party or Parties and the provisions of S 52 of the Act shall apply.

4.4- The XYZ COMMUNITY/SOCIETY shall act as administrator of the arbitration until the point where the Arbitrator is appointed. All communications or notices in writing between the Parties and the XYZ COMMUNITY/SOCIETY prior to the Arbitrator's appointment will be forwarded by the XYZ COMMUNITY/SOCIETY, to the Arbitrator and shall be deemed to be received by him/her at the time of his/her appointment by this society.

5. ARBITRATION PROCEDURES

5.1- It shall be for the Arbitrator to decide all procedural and evidential matters subject to Article 1.3 above.

5.2- before making any application to the Arbitrator for directions as to procedural or evidential matters, a Party must give the other Party a reasonable opportunity (being not less than 15 days unless the Arbitrator otherwise directs), to agree the terms of the directions proposed. Any proposed agreement on directions must be communicated to the Arbitrator for his approval/consideration.

5.3- Any application for directions on procedural or evidential matters, or response thereto must be accompanied by all such evidence or reasoned submissions as the applicant may consider appropriate in the circumstances or as directed by the Arbitrator, and the Arbitrator may determine time limits for making or responding to such applications.

5.4- If in the event the Arbitrator orders that a meeting shall take place, or if one is requested by one or each of the Parties, and the Arbitrator accedes to that request, the Arbitrator will give directions on the format and procedure for such a meeting.

6. POWERS OF THE ARBITRATOR

6.1- The Arbitrator shall have all the powers given to itself by the Act governing such matter,.

6.2- The Arbitrator may limit the number of expert witnesses to be
called by any party, may direct that no expert be called on any issue(s), or state that expert evidence may be called only with the permission of the Arbitrator.

6.3- Where the same Arbitrator is appointed under these Rules in two or more arbitrations which appear to raise common issues of fact or law, and each one of the Parties is common to all the arbitrations, the Arbitrator may direct that such two or more arbitrations or any specific claims or issues arising therein, be consolidated or heard concurrently.

6.4- Where an Arbitrator has ordered consolidation of proceedings or concurrent hearings, he may give such further directions as are necessary or appropriate for the purposes of such consolidated proceedings or concurrent hearings. The Arbitrator may exercise any powers given to him by these Rules or by the Act either separately or jointly in relation thereto.

6.6- Where the Arbitrator orders concurrent hearings, the Arbitrator will, unless the Parties otherwise agree, deliver separate Awards in each arbitration.

6.7- Where an Arbitrator has ordered consolidation or concurrent hearings, he may at any time revoke any orders previously made and give such further orders or directions as may be appropriate for the separate hearing and determination of each arbitration.

6.8- The Arbitrator has power to grant relief on a provisional basis in respect of the following matters:

  a. A provisional order for the payment of money or the disposition of property as between the Parties
  b. A provisional order for interim payment on account of the costs of the arbitration.
  c. A provisional order for the grant of any relief claimed in the arbitration.

6.9- The Arbitrator may exercise the power of granting provisional relief set out in Article 6.8

above on the application of a Party or on his own volition, provided that he gives an opportunity to each Party to make representations in respect thereof.

6.10- The Arbitrator may order any money or property that is the subject of an order for provisional relief to be paid or delivered to a stakeholder on such terms, as he considers appropriate.

6.11- An order for provisional relief may be confirmed, varied or revoked in whole or in part at any time by the arbitrator who made it or by any other Arbitrator who may subsequently have jurisdiction over the dispute to which it relates.

7. FORM OF PROCEDURE

7.1- Subject to the rights of the Parties to agree to adopt a documents-only or some other simplified or expedited procedure and subject to the Arbitrators right to proceed in the absence of a Party in default, each party has the right to be heard before the Arbitrator.

7.2- Unless the Arbitrator otherwise directs, the arbitration will proceed on the basis of statements exchanged as hereinafter set out.

7.3- Statements should contain all allegations of fact or matters of opinion which it is intended to establish by evidence, and set out all items of relief or other remedies sought, together with the total value of all quantifiable sums claimed, and must be signed by or on behalf of the Party submitting the statement. Where a party denies any allegation, it must state the reasons for doing so, and provide its own version.

7.4- Parties should include in any Statement:
a. Details of the specific Acts or case law which they intend to cite.
b. The names and statements of any witnesses of fact;
c. Copies of any other documents that they consider necessary to their claim(s) including any experts' reports.

7.5- Where a claim is based on a written agreement a copy of the Contract or any documents constituting the agreement should be attached to or served with the Statement of Claim.

7.6- Unless the Arbitrator otherwise directs, the Parties will exchange statements as follows:
a. Within 28 Days of the receipt by the Claimant of the Arbitrator's acceptance of the appointment the Claimant shall send

to the Arbitrator and the Respondent its Statement of Claim.

b. The respondent shall within 28 days from the receipt of the Statement of Claim, send to the arbitrator and to the Claimant a Statement of Defence. If no Statement of Defence is served within that time limit or such extended time limit as the Arbitrator may allow, then the Respondent will be debarred from serving a Statement of Defence or having one considered;

c. If the Respondent wishes to make any counterclaim, then a Statement of Counterclaim shall be served with the Statement of Defence.

d. The claimant shall, within 28 days from receipt of the statement(s) of Defence and Counterclaim (if any) sends to the Arbitrator and to the Respondent a reply (and Statement of defence to Counterclaim if any). If neither reply, nor a Statement of Defence to Counterclaim is served within that time limit, or such extended time limit as the Arbitrator may allow, then the Claimant will be debarred from serving a Reply or Statement of Defence to Counterclaim as the case may be.

a) The Respondent shall, within 14 days, send to the arbitrator and to the claimant a Reply to the statement of the Defence to the Counterclaim. If no reply is served within that time limit or such extended time limit as the Arbitrator may allow, then the Respondent will be debarred from serving a Reply.

b) Any further statements may only be served with the leave of the Arbitrator.

c) When a Party has been debarred from serving a Statement of Defence or Statement of Defence to Counterclaim or reply thereto, under Article7.6b 7.6d or 7.6e above, the other Party or Parties shall still be required to prove any allegations made in the Statements of claim, or Counterclaim, as the case may be.

7.7 - At any time, the Arbitrator may give detailed directions with any appropriate timetable for all further procedural steps in the arbitration including (but not limited to) the following:
  a. Any amendment to, expansion of, or reproduction in some other format of any statement, or any extension to or alteration of time limits for statements:

b. Disclosure and production of documents between the Parties;

c. the exchange of statements of evidence of witnesses of fact;

d. The number and types of expert and exchange of their reports;

Meetings between experts;

Arrangements for any hearing;
a) The procedures to be adopted at any hearing;
b) Any time limits to be imposed on the length of oral submissions or the examination or cross-examination of witnesses.

7.8 - The Arbitrator may at any time order any of the following to be delivered to him in writing;
   a. Submissions to be advanced by or on behalf of any party;
   b. Questions intended to be put to any witness;
   c. Answers by any witness to written questions.

8. 8.1 - Any Award shall be in writing, dated, and signed by the Arbitrator, and shall contain sufficient reasons to show why the Arbitrator has reached the decisions contained in it, unless the Parties otherwise agree or the ward is by consent.

8.2 - In the first instance, the Arbitrator may submit an Award or a proposal to the Parties in draft form and may in his discretion consider any further written submissions or proposals put to him by any Party, but subject to any time limit that he may impose.

8.3 Any Award shall state the seat of the arbitration.

9. COSTS

9.1 - The general principle is that the losing Party shall pay costs, but the Arbitrator has an overriding discretion to decide whether or not to apportion the costs having regard to all material circumstances, including such of the following as may be relevant:

a) Which (if any) of the issues raised in the arbitration has led to the incurring of substantial costs and which party succeeded in respect of such issues.

b) Whether any claim which succeeded was unreasonably exaggerated;

c) The conduct of the Party which succeeded with any claim(s) and any concession(s) made by the other Party.

d) D. Degree of success of each Party;

e) Any admissible evidence of any offer or settlement or compromise made by any Party.

9.2 - In considering any admissible evidence of any offer of settlement or compromise by any Party (whether such offer was made before or after the commencement of the arbitration), the Arbitrator shall normally follow the principle that a Party who is Awarded the same as, or less than was offered overall or for any specific issue, should recover the costs otherwise recoverable only up to the date when it was reasonable that such offer should have been accepted and the Party making the offer should recover its costs thereafter with respect to any matters covered by such offer.

10. REVIEW OF AWARD.

10.1 - The Arbitrator has discretion if either Party makes any application within 28 days of the Award to;
   a) Correct the Award so as to remove a clerical error arising from an accidental slip, an omission, or to clarify/remove any ambiguity in the award, or
   b) B. Make an additional Award in respect of any claim or counterclaim (including one

for interest or costs) which was presented to the Arbitrator but was not dealt with in the Award.

10.2 - Before exercising the discretion given in Para 10.1, the Arbitrator will give the other Party or Parties a reasonable opportunity to make representations on the application.

10.3 - The arbitrator shall make any necessary correction of Award within 28 days of the receipt of the application, whilst any additional award will be made within 30 days of the receipt of such an application.

11. APPEALS AGAINST AWARD TO THE NATIONAL XYZ COMMUNITY/SOCIETY

11.1 - Any Party may Appeal the arbitrator's award subject to the following provisions:

a. The Applicant must have exhausted the review of Arbitration mechanism (if applicable) as provided by paragraph 10.

b. The Appeal must be made within 28 days of the date of Award or of the date of notification of the result of the review mechanism as provided in Para 10, which will be deemed for this purpose to be the date of publication of the Award.

c. An Appeal can only be made on a point of law and/or on the grounds that based on the findings of fact in the Award the decision of the Arbitrator is obviously wrong and/or on the grounds that there has been a serious irregularity affecting the Arbitrator, the proceedings or the Award.

12. COSTS OF APPEAL

12.1 - The National XYZ COMMUNITY/SOCIETY may make an Award allocating the costs of the Appeal as between the Parties but shall Award costs on the general principle that costs should follow the event. The recoverable costs of the Appeal shall be determined on the basis of a reasonable amount of costs reasonably incurred.

13. GENERAL

13.1 - Any Party may be represented by any person or persons of their choice subject to such proof of authority as the Arbitrator may require.

13.2 - The Arbitrator shall establish and record the addresses, telephone/fax numbers as well as e-mail addresses of each Party and their respective representatives.

13.4 - The parties shall inform the Arbitrator promptly of any proposed application to the court and shall provide him with copies of all documentation intended to be used in any such application.

APPENDIX 6

SAMPLE ARBITRATION CLAUSES

Credit to Encyclopedia of forms and precedents, J: m lightwood M.A.

1. CLAUSE for insertion in any Instrument for referring Future Differences to Arbitration. - General

All questions or differences whatsoever which shall at any time hereafter arise between the parties hereto or their respective representatives or any of them touching or concerning this deed [agreement] or the construction meaning operation or effect thereof or of any clause herein contained or as to the rights duties or liabilities of the parties hereto respectively or their respective representatives or any of them under or by virtue of this deed [agreement] or otherwise or touching the subject-matter hereof or arising out of or in relation thereto shall be referred to a single arbitrator to be agreed upon by the parties hereto and in accordance with and subject to the provisions of the Arbitration Acts any statutory modification on re-enactment thereof the time being in force.
The respective parties hereto will, in the event of a dispute, do and cause to be done all things necessary and convenient for enabling the arbitrator to make his award without delay.

2. AGREEMENT to refer all Existing Differences to a Single Arbitrator.

Disputes and differences have arisen between the parties touching the arbitrator shall have all the powers given to arbitrators by the Arbitration Acts and shall make his award under his hand on or before the --- day of --- next or within such extended time not exceeding --- months after that day as he said arbitrator shall by writing under his hand appoint.
The parties hereto have agreed to refer the said matters to arbitration.

WE herby agree that [arbitrator] of etc, shall decide all matters in difference between us and to that end shall have all the powers given by the Arbitration Acts to Arbitrators and may direct either us to do or submit to any act or to sign or execute any instrument and may obtain such professional and expert assistance and may give such directions in his award as he deems fit.

3. CLAUSE for ARBITRATION in a Partnership Deed.

All disputes and questions whatsoever which shall either during the partnership or afterwards arise between the partners or their respective representatives or between any partners or partner and the representatives of any other or others touching this deed or the construction or application thereof or any clause or thing herein contained or any account valuation or division of assets debts or liabilities to be made hereunder or as to any act deed or omission of any partner or as to any person hereunder shall be referred to a single arbitrator in accordance with and subject to the provisions of the Arbitration acts or any statutory modification thereof for the time being in force.

Disputes and differences have arisen between the parties touching the arbitrator shall have all the powers given to arbitrators by the Arbitration Acts and shall make his award under his hand on or before the --- day of --- next or within such extended time not exceeding --- months after that day as he said arbitrator shall by writing under his hand appoint.

The parties hereto have agreed to refer the said matters to arbitration.

The respective parties hereto will do and cause to be done all things necessary and convenient for enabling the arbitrator to make his award without delay.

4. CLAUSE for ARBITRATION in a Building Contract.

All disputes or questions which shall either during the progress of the works or after their completion arise between the parties hereto or their respective representatives or between the one party and the representatives of the other concerning the works or the execution or maintenance thereof or the construction or meaning hereof or the specifications drawings plans instructions or directions hereinbefore referred to or as any other matter arising out of or connected with or incidental to this contract or the works to be executed or payments to be made in pursuance thereof or the rights duties pr obligations of any person in relation to the premised shall be referred to the Arbitration Acts or any statutory modification thereof the time being in force. Disputes and differences have arisen between the parties touching the arbitrator shall have all the powers given to arbitrators by the Arbitration Acts and shall make his award under his hand on or before the --- day of --- next or within such extended time not exceeding --- months after that day as he said arbitrator shall by writing under his hand appoint.

The parties hereto have agreed to refer the said matters to arbitration.

The respective parties hereto will do and cause to be done all things necessary and convenient for enabling the arbitrator to make his award without delay.

5. REFERENCE by Deed to Arbitrators, Disputes under Lease

THIS DEED is made etc, BETWEEN [landlord] of etc (hereinafter called the landlord) of the one part and [Tenant] of etc. (hereinafter called tenant) of the other part.

Wheras

By the lease dated --- and made between the landlord of the one part and the tenant of the other part the landlord demised to the tenant a house situate at --- in the country of --- for a term of --- years commencing on the day of --- [or as tenant from year to year from the

--- day of ---] at the yearly rent of --- and subject to the convents conditions and stipulations therein contained. The said tenancy expired by passage of time [or by notice for quit on the --- day off ---.

Disputes have arisen between the parties hereto respecting alleged breaches of the several stipulations contained in the said lease and as to mutual claims by the parties hereto against each other arising there out and in particular the landlord claims damages against the tenant for not yielding up the house and building in good repair.

NOW THIS DEED WITHNESSETH that it is agreed between the parties hereto as follows:

All questions in difference between the parties touching the matters hereinbefore in recital mentioned and all other questions arising out of the said lease or tenancy hitherto subsisting between the parties hereto or otherwise howsoever are hereby referred to the award and final determination of [first arbitrator] of etc and [second arbitrator] of etc.

The parties hereto and their respective representatives will in all respects aside by observe perform and obey the said award so to be made and published as aforesaid.

The parties respectively will do al acts necessary to enable the arbitrators or their umpire to make their or his award herein and neither of them will willfully or wrongfully do or cause to be done any act to delay or prevent the arbitrators or their umpire from making their or his award

Neither of the parties shall bring or prosecute any action against the other or against the arbitrators or their umpire or either for or in respect of the said matters in difference or any or either of them or for or in respect of the said award to be made in pursuance of this submission.

6. Clauses in an AGREEMENT by Executers to refer
   disputed Claims against the Estate of their Testator.

AN AGREEMENT made etc. Between [executers] of etc., of the one part and [creditor] of etc of the other part

Whereas

The said [executers] are the executers of the will of [testator] late of etc. dated --- and proved in the --- Probate Registry.

The said[creditor] claim that the said [testator]was at the time of his death and that his estate still is indebted to the said [creditor]in the sum of --- for moneys from time to time advanced and lent to the said [testator] and for work and labour done

Disputes have arisen touching the liability of the estate of the said [testator] in respect of such claims

In pursuance of the statuary power © behalf the said [executers] have agreed to submit the said claims to arbitration in manner hereinafter expressed.

NOW IT IS HERBY AGREED between the parties hereto as follows:

The said claims and all matters in questions between the parties hereto relating the premises are hereby referred to the award and final determination of [arbitrator] of etc. This agreement is entered into by the said [executers] respectively as the personal representatives of the said [testator] and shall not create any personal responsibility on the part of the said [executers] or either of them. This agreement shall not be deemed to be an admission by the said [executers] that they have assets of the said testator sufficient to satisfy the award to be made.

7. Clauses for arbitration in a PRENUP AGREEMENT
We hereby agree that in the event of a dispute or difference arising in relation to the marriage, including matters relating to children of the family and matrimonial property, we will submit the dispute or difference to—for mediation, and in the event that mediation does not result in a settlement within 60 days, the unresolved portion of the dispute or difference shall automatically be referred to arbitration by --- in accordance with its rules of procedure in effect at the time of such referral.

The parties respectively will do al acts necessary to enable the arbitrator's or their umpire to make their or his award herein and neither of them will willfully or wrongfully do or cause to be done any act to delay or prevent the arbitrators or their umpire from making their or his award.

10. CLAUSES for ARBITRATION in a company constitution

All disputes and questions whatsoever which shall either during the existence of the company or afterwards arise between the directors or shareholders or their respective representatives or others touching this constitution or Memorandum and Articles of Association or the construction or application thereof or any clause or thing herein contained or any account valuation or division of assets debts or liabilities to be made hereunder or as to any act deed or omission of any director, shareholder or as to any person hereunder shall be referred to a single arbitrator in accordance with and subject to the provisions of the Arbitration acts or any statutory modification thereof for the time being in force.

The respective parties hereto will do and cause to be done all things necessary and convenient for enabling the arbitrator to make his award without delay.

CREDITS

My daughter Naveeda Keshavjee (Bachelor of Arts Honours, Political science and Psychology-Queens University) for transcribing, formatting, proofreading

Institute of Arbitrators of UK.

Mustill and Boyd, Commercial Arbitration 2nd edition Butterworths

Encyclopaedia of forms and precedents Jm Lightwood Ma

Alberta and Arbitration Mediation Society

Gary Zukav "Daily Reflection for spiritual Growth"

Jonette Watson Hamilton associate professor faculty of law U of C.

Ethan Katsh and Janet Rifkin - "online Dispute Resolution" 2001

The power of an apology from" Conflict resolution today March 2006"
("A conversation Between Evita Rogie and Neil Sargent")

Wayne Dyer—(various lectures)

Aga Khan International Conciliation and Arbitration Board

Aga Khan Development Network www.Akdn.org

Dr Mohammad Keshavjee Lecture at world mediation forum, Argentina.

Marion Boyd - former Attorney General from her 2004 paper 'dispute resolution in family law: protecting choice promoting inclusion

My friend Nadim Kurji BA LL.B (Hon) for proofreading and valuable comments.

My Neighbour Faizan Manji for transcribing

Professor Amyn Sajoo, founding editor of publications at the IIS

Javid Nasseri, BA, MA candidate, critical disability studies York University